In the name of God

***

Unwithering Flames: Book-2 "Shahid Daqayeqi; Narrated by His Wife" by: Ali Maraj
Copyright © 2023 Ali Maraj

All rights reserved. No portion of this book may be reproduced in any form without permission from the publisher. For permissions contact: info@Greenpalm.net
Translated and edited by: Green Palm books
Cover by Hossein Reza Vanaki
First Edition

To contribute in the publishing process and be informed about other volumes of the series, please contact info@Greenpalm.net

Unwithering Flames

—— Book 2 - Ismail Daqayeqi ——

In order to have a fruitful and prosperous relationship, people have come to the realization that they must love one another. Unfortunately, the meaning of true love has been lost. Many have relegated love to just intimacy between a man and a woman. However, this is just the initial stage of true love, and we must aspire to reach a higher level beyond mere physical attraction. Such love is built on the foundation of honesty, enjoyment, selflessness, and spiritual attainment. Although many strive to reach this transcendent form of love, the affairs of this world become a barrier for them.

This series of books entitled Unwithering Flames recounts to us stories of those men and women who in the events of the Islamic Revolution and the Iran-Iraq War turned away from this world, just for the sake of God. In doing so, they became lovers in the true sense. They had the kind of love that did not only make the pain of this world bearable, rather it was something beautiful for them. The love, whose flame has not dimmed even with martyrdom or death.

🌐 www.GREENPALM.net

📞 +98 999 99 16 140

✉ info@GREENPALM.net

Ismail Daqayeqi

Birth: 29th of June, 1954
Admission to the University of Ahvaz: 1974
Admission to the University of Tehran: 1976
Married to Masoumeh Hamrahi: 3rd of June, 1979
Martyrdom: 18th of January, 1987 (Shalamcheh)

SYNOPSIS

The love story between Masoumeh and Ismail Daqayeqi is destined to last until the gates of heaven. Masoumeh's mother used to say, "I had given my daughter to a student, but he turned out to be a soldier." Masoumeh, however, loved this soldier. Her wedding and union coincided with the Revolution of Iran. Their lives were entangled with restlessness and moving from one city to another. This was especially so after the war had erupted. Ismail asked God not to make any two days of their lives like one another. He also hoped that Masoumeh would wish for the same. He did not like their couple life to be broken apart by dragging through long years; and he was lucky as there was a war going on.

After his martyrdom, when Masoumeh read his will, it stated, "If heaven is in my destiny, I will wait for you there by the gates." She did not wish to complain about the world after Ismail. However, she used to always say, "I am now awaiting my turn so that Ismail does not wait for me for too long.

Contents

Chapter 1
The Sacred Cause, From Aghajari to Tehran...9

Chapter 2
An Unexpected Proposal.....................................31

Chapter 3
Living Next to the Frontline..............................43

Chapter 4
A Commander Only Outside the House..........57

Chapter 5
Ahvaz, Our Last Reunion...................................77

Chapter 1

The Sacred Cause, From Aghajari to Tehran

The English had smelled the scent of oil and constructed a small city for them to drill from. One could not call it a city exactly; a few houses were built in the middle of the desert for the company workers who had traveled from the other cities of "Khuzestan"¹ province for employment. They named the city "Aghajari."

---

1. Khuzestan is a province in southwestern Iran. The province is located on the shores of the Persian Gulf and Arvand River (or *Shatt al-Arab*), and most of its residents are Arabs and Lors. Khuzestan was the main field of the Iraqi war against Iran. Early after the war, Iraq occupied parts of this province and launched missile and arsenal attacks on its cities, which resulted in considerable damages to their infrastructures.

> *The residential complex was just like any other complex; that was constructed in fertile areas to plunder the locals' resources. A line of houses, a line of stores, and people unaffiliated with one another, who had to work all day to make ends meet. Earlier on, houses had not been constructed, so the workers had to live in tents. Later, when a market was constructed and the need for more workforce had become eminent, they advertised that anybody who would go to live and work in that area would be granted a house to live in. The family's breadwinners would go from "Behbahan"[2] to work there; some of them were tailors, and the oil company contracted them to sew clothes for their employees.*

I was a third-grader when we decided to move out of Behbahan. Our family lived in Behbahan and my father would come home from Aghajari every once in a while, to check up on us. My mother had grown tired of living far away from my father and decided that we needed to move to the city

---

 2. Behbahan is a city in the southeast of Khuzestan Province.

where my father worked and lived. At first, when we arrived in Aghajari, I was shocked when I saw women were not covering their hair and had no *hijab* on the streets. The atmosphere there was based on the English and its oil company's culture. Many of my father's customers were Englishmen. Even some of the words people used in their daily language were in English.

Our house was one of the houses designated for the shopkeepers who worked at the market. It was located just behind the shop; it was a small house intended for simple workers. Life in Aghajari was more challenging than living in Behbahan; as the weather in Behbahan was better. However, the weather in Aghajari had the resemblance to the hot weather in the south but without its humidity. The city was stationed in the middle of the desert and the wind would bring all the sand and dust into the city. Despite the heat, we did not have an air conditioner. We had to improvise and use a makeshift air conditioner using a fan, water and straw. On the other hand, we were provided with all kinds of heating equipment. There was no fee for gas, but it was unfiltered, and the stove was always on in the kitchen, as we used it to warm up the water for the bathtub.

As the family's youngest daughter, I had a particular position in my parent's eyes. They kept telling me, "You brought us good luck, and God granted us a son after your arrival." We were a large family; we were six daughters and two sons who were born after me. The only fun we had in a city like that was visiting our relatives and their houses. My aunt's family had moved to Aghajari a few years prior to us. They were also a large family, but unlike us, they had five sons and two daughters. Our cousins were the only children we had the chance to speak and play with, as we were all in the same age range. Either they would spend time in our house, or we would go to their house. My cousins were like my brothers. As far as I recall from my teenage years, I seemed like a shy, innocent, and calm girl, unlike Ismail, my cousin, who was a naughty and energetic boy. Ismail was the second-born son of the family and always caused trouble, unlike his elder brother, who was very calm.

Ismail was only fifteen or sixteen years old when he got accepted in the vocational school in the city of Ahvaz.[3] The school was funded by the oil company. Attending a school that provided free boarding alongside a free education was a high achievement. Ismail's mindset and character were already shaped after attending school and leaving for Ahvaz. Prior to that, I can only recall his childish behavior in the alleyway and at the house. However, after going to that school in Ahvaz, he learned things that were not taught in our small city of Aghajari. He started reading books as well. He would buy all the new books that were published. If he were to give a gift to someone, it would undoubtedly be a book. The first books he ever bought were written by Samad Behrangi, who bluntly talked about controversial topics. He brought me the book "The Little Black Fish," which greatly influenced me. His mother would jokingly call him Mulla Ismail as he always talked about the books he read. On every weekend picnic that the two families went on, you could see Ismail was no longer the same child I grew up with. He would talk about "Resistance" and "school of thought." As relatives, we had a very close relationship,

---

3. Ahvaz is a major historical city in Iran and the capital of Khuzestan Province in southwestern Iran.

and it was natural for me to be interested in what he had to say. During the holidays, when he returned from Ahvaz to Aghajari, he would bring my siblings and me some books. We would wait for his arrival each time to see which new books we would be given. He was the reason we got to know authors like Jalal Al Ahmad,[4] Shariati,[5] and Morteza Motahhari.[6] Carrying such books would be considered treason, but our parents, who were not big fans of the monarchy, did not mind if we read the books Ismail would bring us.

In Ahvaz Vocational School, he made the acquaintance of Mohsen Rezaee.[7] This late

---

4. Jalal Al-e-Ahmad (1923-1969) was a well-known Iranian fiction writer and intellectual, who criticized the Pahlavi regime and the Westernization of Iranian intellectuals in his works.
5. Dr. Ali Shariati (1933-1977) was a well-known Iranian intellectual and dissident and a theorist of anti-colonialism and anti-tyranny.
6. Ayatollah Shaheed Morteza Motahhari(1298-1358) was an Iranian author, a seminary and university professor of Islamic philosophy and theology in Iran, a prominent student of Imam Khomeini and Allameh Tabatabaee who was assassinated and martyred at the hands of the terrorist group, Forqan.
7. Mohsen Rezaee (born 1954) was a senior commander of the Islamic Revolutionary Guard Corps during the Iraq's war against Iran.

acquaintance was the beginning of his fight against the monarch regime. There were about four or five classmates that arrived to this conclusion that the government did not deserve to be in power and that drove them to take up some actions. To begin with, they would hold sessions to recite the Holy Quran in their dorms. One of the duties in their little organization was to preach the message of resistance to others around them. Although Islam was the country's official religion, one could not see any signs of it in the society.

Aghajari had a mosque that nobody attended, and it was a gathering place for the elderly. There was nobody to teach the people essential matters of religion and politics. Ismail scheduled meetings in the mosque to recite and discuss the last short chapters of the Holy Quran. Most of the youngsters in the city would attend these gatherings. He would talk about the aspects that were appealing to the youth. He would say, "The regime wants to keep the youth occupied with unimportant matters so nobody would notice how the foreigners are plundering their country." This was something we could see with our own eyes as well. The English and Americans were our masters, and we were servants in our own country. Ismail had shifted the atmosphere of the mosque from a place that nobody would attend to a hangout spot for the local youngsters. Sometimes when he returned from Ahvaz, he would go to his father's shop with his friends late at night. Later we realized that they were printing manifestos[8] using an old printing machine.

The "Savak"[9] intelligence service grew suspicious of their Quran meetings in the vocational school. Especially when Ismail and his friends left the dormitory and rented a house. They did things that resulted in dire consequences if Savak became aware. These things included placing a handmade

---

8. Since November 1964 to February 1979, the Pahlavi regime exiled Imam Khomeini to Najaf and then France. During this period, he issued manifestos in which he expressed his position and led people's campaigns against the Pahlavi regime. The manifestos were written by Imam Khomeini and then conveyed to revolutionaries, who then published and duplicated them.

9. Intelligence and Security Organization of Country, abbreviated as SAVAK, was the security institute of the Pahlavi regime, which was founded in 1957 under the support and planning of the US, to enhance the monitoring of political dissidents and with the motto of "protecting the safety of the country."

bomb in the Reza Khan[10] monument (for which the trigger was not activated) or the interruption of the programs of a circus that was in the south in honor of the king.

It was 1973; they were in the third year of the Vocational School when Savak arrested all of them at once. The Savak agents simply marched into their workshop, apprehended them all, and sent them straight to prison while still in their workshop uniforms. We were all worried for them as they were not even adults yet. They were each in solitary confinement without the right to have any visitors. Savak kept them in prison for two months and finally released them. They held Mohsen Rezaee for a while longer in prison, however. Upon their return, they were all expelled from school with an excuse of "extended absenteeism from classes."

Prison made a man out of him; it was clear to see. It was a chance for him to apply the knowledge he had gained from reading those books. When he was released from prison, he first went to a friend's house and then came to visit us as if nothing had happened. He did not want to allow Savak

---

10. Reza Pahlavi (1878-1944), known as Reza Shah or Reza Khan, was the founder of the Pahlavi Dynasty.

to instill fear in everyone's hearts. He told us it was in prison that he learned the truth about the regime. He would say that it is nothing but a paper tiger. Our oppressors have more bark than bite. He said, "We just need to educate ourselves and work in the shadows to evade them." He would respond in sarcasm to the elders of the family, who were always worried about him and believed he was playing with fire. He would tell them that he had learned many things in prison, for instance, how one could entertain himself with vermin and mice and learn how to sleep in a cell that was not even big enough for sitting. His imprisonment had turned into a badge of honor for us as we could brag about the fact that we had a fighter in our family. Ismail, who once was a playmate of mine, had turned into an adult much faster than any of us.

When Ismail was expelled from the school, he returned to Aghajari and stayed with his family to prepare for the university entrance exams. When he was a student at the vocational school, he would attend the workshops and classes in the morning and study the mathematics books taught in the high school at night. He achieved his mathematics diploma in Ahvaz and was really good at mathematics. From the time he returned to Aghajari to prepare and study for the entrance exam, he worked as a tutor to help his family with the expenses. His student network grew in numbers very quickly. During the session breaks, if he saw that the students had some potential, he would speak about politics with them. He was always busy with lessons and studying during those days, and then he eventually got accepted in water engineering at the university of "Jundi Shapoor" in Ahvaz.

I was in high school at that time. We could take an exam to enter a community college in ninth grade. If we were accepted and studied well enough, we would have a chance to be hired to teach at schools. I was accepted in the entrance exam and went to Ahvaz. The way people dressed and covered themselves back then was much different from now. We would cover our heads with a colorful veil and not wear any scarves underneath it. In the south, because many foreigners would come and go, the concept of having a full *hijab* was not very common. It was not easy for a young boy to approach a girl and tell her: "It would suit you better if you had a scarf underneath your veil," but he would also say, "Do not pay attention to those who make fun of you. You have to learn how to fight for your beliefs, and this is your first step." His words motivated me to put on a scarf. I was five years younger than him and looked up to him as a big brother who was more experienced and really knew what he was doing or talking about. Since that day, every time he wanted to enter our house, he would announce his entrance by calling out, "*Ya Allah.*" At first, it was not easy for me to understand what I was supposed to do. Later I realized "*Ya Allah*" meant that we had to have a proper *hijab* so he could enter the house. He had asked the same things from the other relatives, but they did not take him seriously. To cover yourself in full *hijab* was not a common thing in Aghajari. In the coming year, I went through a lot of trouble for practicing *hijab* at the college as well. The dean would sarcastically say: "Maybe you are bald and prefer that nobody sees your skull." However, I did not care for their words.

Ismail had taken his political activities to a bigger scale but still kept them hidden. I remember once he took all his wages in the summer and went to a village in "Bandar Abbas" and built a library there. He created a bookfair in "Behbahan" as well. He also helped me gather a few girls in Aghajari's mosque to perform some religious activities. His point of view had affected my perspective on life entirely as well. I had turned into the "small black fish" who wanted to swim against the river's current. Perhaps it was customary to change so much at that age. However, it was not merely the excitement of adolescence and the teenage years. We could see the other youth and how they spent their days. We believed there had to be a higher purpose than having materialistic values and living a mediocre life. We believed that humans were entitled to greatness. All that excitement led to three failed courses at the college. He was so disappointed over the news that he encouraged me to study harder, so hard that I got A's in all those courses and turned into one of the top students in the class thereafter.

Now that he had become a university student, he would motivate us to pursue our education further and enter a university. The certificate they provided at the community college was not deemed as a diploma, though, so we could not take the entrance exam. Ismail insisted that I should not be satisfied with a community college degree. He would say, "As long as you are not a university student, you cannot take the fight to the regime." After two years of graduation from the college, he insisted on me studying the mathematics books and preparing for the university entrance exam. I had to reenroll in high school and sit with my old classmates again. He helped me a lot on my journey. Later on, he concluded that he needed to take the human science exam and change his major. He wanted to get accepted into a new university in a bigger city like Tehran to be more politically active. He needed to study some of the human science books, and that he did. We both got accepted in the same year in the university entrance exam. He got accepted at the University of Tehran in educational sciences and I, due to an error, in geology at the same university. When I was choosing the universities, I had mistakenly put in the wrong code for my major and ended up in Tehran instead of the university of Ahvaz, a mistake that changed my fate.

Now we were both in the heart of the city of Tehran, as though we were fishes newly arrived at the sea. Tehran completely had the capacity to change the destinies of two youngsters like us, who had left a conservative city like Aghajari. We were able to attend and listen to the lectures of those very writers whose books we used to secretly exchange; such as Dr. Shariati, Shaheed Motahhari and so on. What else could we ask for? Ismail pointed out, "Simply being against the regime is not enough." The students who were against the regime were divided into two groups: those whose school of thoughts were based on Islam and those of communism. After entering the university, we joined the Islamic association at the university; it was a hangout spot for the religious students to gather and exchange their thoughts.

I became accustomed to living in a new city very quickly. Perhaps it was because I was used to living in a dormitory since I entered the community college. We would hold Quran recitation sessions in the dormitory with a few other girls. When the dormitory dean saw that we were not the type of girls who would go to movie theatres or do make-up like the others, she grew suspicious of our actions. She reported us, and we were expelled from the dormitory. The girls and I looked for an apartment and were able to rent a house on Forsat street with only six hundred tomans[11] as the Security deposit and thirty tomans as rent. I told my family that the dormitory was not comfortable enough for studying. Our house was an old tiny unit in the basement of an old house, but at least we were comfortable and free to conduct our sessions without worrying about being sold down the river. My interaction with Ismail was still the same way. He would come to collect me, and we would attend a meeting or a lecture together. I would tell him about the problems a single and lonely girl had in a far city from home, and he would watch over me as a friend. Back then, we both would tutor to have some cash in hand and occasionally share our earnings.

Although we did not have a regular schedule to meet up and would not see him that often, I still recalled some news of his whereabouts and what he did from here and there. Ismail and a few other students had turned into black sheep students who were radically against the regime. He was a senior member of the Islamic association at the university, and they were drafting a constitution.

---

11. The Iranian currency.

It was customary to fall behind on following the lessons when one did so many extra-curricular activities. However, it was not just studying at a university and the education that helped me tolerate the distance from my family. Back then, the universities had a different lively vibe to them, and it was not just lessons and assignments that kept one busy. Ismail had made connections at the revolutionary organizations outside the university as well. Mohsen Rezaee, who had been evading Savak agents for years by using fake IDs, was also in Tehran. He and Ismail kept in touch. They were both members of the "Mansoroon" organization; a militia branch of the Islamic Revolutionary fighters.

Ismail did not study his lessons for over a year and was expelled from the university eventually; he was forbidden to go back to classes for at least two semesters and charged with carrying out the ideology of Imam Khomeini. He was also under surveillance because they knew he had a fire in his heart. This gave him an ease of mind to fully dedicate himself to his fight against the regime as he had no other responsibilities. He had information about all of the actions taken against the regime.

He would participate in the demonstrations and distribute the flyers of Imam Khomeini's manifestos. Sometimes we would go back to the south together. He had created a library in our neighborhood's mosque and would donate some books each time we went back to visit our families. He also opened a book fair that many people attended.

> *It was prevalent for students to go mountain climbing. The peace and tranquility enabled them to discuss the matters they could not simply discuss at the university. All the anthems students used to sing in the mountains were political and religious due to society's limitations. He used to go to the mountains with eight of his old classmates. They would go up to the mountains and read the interpretation of Ayatollah Taleghani[12] on Surah "wa*

12. Ayatollah Sayyid Mahmoud Taleghani (1911-1979) was an Iranian religious scholar who spent many years of his life, fighting against the Pahlavi regime, and was thus frequently imprisoned and tortured by the regime. In addition to his political activities, he taught *Nahj al-Balaghah* and Quranic exegesis. The six-volume book, *Partuwi az Quran* (A ray from the Quran), is his exegesis of the Quran, which remained unfinished due to his demise.

l-Asr". They could not carry any books with them, so they would write down the points of the books on their hands or pieces of paper. Ismail had given me a piece of advice when he was freed from prison when we were teenagers: "Fighting in the Shadows".

One day, when we were climbing up a mountain, we saw about thirty people in suits carrying a red piece of cloth in their hands and chanting "death to the Shah" and walking down the mountain. They did not look like students at all. At first, we thought they were some sort of thugs that one could see everywhere around the city during that time, but when they got closer and started interrogating the students, the students realized that they were Savak agents. They were chanting and singing revolutionary slogans to manipulate the younger and less experienced into joining them to find an excuse to seize them all. Ismail gestured to the rest of the group to keep silent to find a way to thwart them. The men in a suit started interrogating us with questions like, "why have you come to this mountain?" and "How many times have you come here before?" I tried to act like an innocent girl, unaware of the things they asked. However, it did not work. The agents seized everyone and took us up the mountain from the same path we were descending. At the mountain's peak, we realized how serious the situation was. The agents had landed at the mountain's peak and were seizing everyone in the area. Some other students were sitting there with their hands and eyes tied up. The agents tied everyone's eyes with the red cloth they were carrying, pushed everyone into the helicopters and took us to a camp in the mountains. There were many captured civilians that were all held in a hall. After that, the group was taken to a prison dedicated to the anti-sabotage committee.

They continued to interrogate the students over and over again. Amongst the captured, there was a fifteen-year-old boy who exemplified a lot of courage. He kept saying, "Your end is at hand, and you think you can save yourselves by instilling fear in people's hearts." All the prisoners were freed a day after. I was praying that the newspapers would not publish our names. I could imagine my mother's face when she would read my name on the papers as an activist against the government. Perhaps she would whine and say, "Her rebellious cousin Ismail is all to blame."

They captured Ismail once again in 1977. I was supposed to meet him at the faculty to be informed about the timing of a speech, but he did not show up. They did not hold him in captivity for a long time. They were looking for Mohsen Rezaee, but he did not budge. Prison is a sort of place that people rarely visit. However, once there, you have a lot of time to think about important matters. You are always given a chance to contemplate your decisions and might even come to the conclusion that you have made a mistake, things were not supposed to materialize like that, and it was better to call that disgusting interrogator who shaved his face twice a day and tell him, "Dear Sir I have made a mistake. I have decided to live like the rest of the society." There is nobody in prison to vouch for your valor or even see your sacrifices. It is very difficult to remain a hero in prison.

During those days, Tehran was very crowded and chaotic. The fight against the regime was taken out to the streets, and it was no longer a fight that needed to be carried out in the shadows. People were openly showing their discontent against the Shah. I was in front of the university on the

13th of Aban[13]. I wanted to attend a class, but I saw a crowd gathered in front of the university. The students had taken each other's hands and formed a line there. Half of them would yell: "Say it," and the rest would respond: "Death to the Shah." I was watching the whole scene from the window of a two-floored bus. Ismail was behind the closed doors of the university and was hitting the guards with a stone. The guards pushed forward and gave the crowd an ultimatum to stop with the slogans. The crowd did not heed their warnings, so they opened fire and martyred a few young high school students in the crowd. When we met at night, he said, "We tried so hard to convince the kids to leave the scene, but they did not listen." He said, "If we as university students were the spearhead of the revolutionary fight, now the revolutionary spirit has reached the hearts of the men, women, and children, and the fighters like us have to run to catch up with the revolutionary train."

---

13. Aban 13 (November 4) is known in Iran as Pupil's Day and the Day of Fighting Imperialism, On this day in 1978 (three months before the victory of the Islamic Revolution), school students in Tehran gathered in the University of Tehran to protest the policies of the Pahlavi regime. Military forces of the regime attacked the students, killing fifty-six and injuring many.

Chapter 2

An Unexpected Proposal

During the unrest, Ismail would update me on the ongoing events. Sometimes he would bring Imam Khomeini's manifestos and update me with some news on the current events in a specific area. We were more like a brother and sister in arms than cousins. The first time we talked about a relationship was in the winter of 1978. I went to see my family with a few of my classmates during the spring break. Ismail booked us a whole cabin in a train. He was accompanying us as well. When we got home, he said that he wanted to propose to me. At that time, all I thought about was the revolution, so I got truly offended. I deemed it taboo for cousins to have feelings for each other. I kept thinking about other people's judgmental opinions. I told him, "If you had such a feeling, you should not have let us grow so close." He said, "One cannot predict or control such things." Before we could unravel the situation, my brother-in-law was martyred while carrying flyers in Ahvaz and left my sister with a newborn baby.

This incident created an atmosphere whereby such matters were not discussed anymore for a while. It seemed like our fate was tied to the revolution's fate after all.

> *She was afraid of getting married to a relative, and She was worried that it might cause their children to be born with defects. She was also worried about her family and their opinions; She knew it would be hard for her mother to allow her daughter to be married to a militia member. Her mother would say, "You cannot have a normal life with a person like him. Each day you have to pack your things and move from one place to another. This boy is fully involved with the revolution, and you will end up just like your sister. At least wait to see how the revolution would go. Even if things go well, do not count on being beside him." Her father had given his approval as he was a relative,*

and they knew him well, but he would say, "People like him are not meant to stay in this world for too long."

However, she believed that such things were decided beforehand. A special feeling that one gets in the heart. The answer of "Yes" which was intended for him from the beginning, and life itself officially wanted them as a couple. Such was the way of life and death, and she ought not worry about it too much.

I kept a distance from him for a while. I would not even answer his phone calls. It took me a year and a few months since the first time he confessed he had feelings for me, to accept his proposal. I do not know why it took me so long. During that time, he would come and bring me some traditions and religious quotes to show that it was okay for relatives to get married. He said such marriages even caused the positive traits of the couple to be strengthened in their children. Some other times, he would ask other people to come and try to get my approval.

He came one last time to give me an ultimatum. He said, "Masoumeh, you know very well that the reason for my decision is not merely based on your appearance and looks. There are countless girls out there. If you truly do not want us to be together, just let me know so I can stop bothering you with my request." I had to come clean to myself and make a decision. I had seen a quote from the religious Imams (or he had shown it to me) that if you had a proposal from a suitor who was a man of faith and well mannered, rejecting someone like that would lead to unforeseen misfortune. I could not find any reasons to reject him, so finally, I gave him my consent. I was really content with my decision as well. After that point, he insisted on getting engaged quickly, so we could be comfortable with one another when we were alone. We went to a cleric that he knew, and he announced us as *Mahram*. Maybe he thought my parents would regret their decision if we did not act quickly enough. Although I knew my mother had her reservation, I accepted to share my life with him. However, I still lived in that shared apartment on Forsat street with my friends. But we used to meet each other more often and also in private. I remember sitting on his motorcycle and going around the city. We were happy to be together, a sort of happiness that all of the chaos in Tehran would add to its excitement.

Once, when we were returning to the south together, he handed me a package before mounting the train and asked me: "Please keep this safe for me." I asked what it was but he did not say anything. I put it inside my bag and he did not ask for it until we reached home. When I handed him the package he said: "Did you know what this was?" The package was full of thousands of handouts of the Imam's manifestoes and a gun. I was shocked. I said, "Did you even know what was in the package?" and made a joke: "So all the rush for getting engaged was to use me to carry such things for you." He smiled and sarcastically agreed. Later he used the gun to train us. He was one of the "Mansooroon" Islamic Revolutionary militia members. For his membership, we had been interrogated in prison a thousand times. We would sit in their house, and he would show me how to open a gun and close it up. It was a kind of revolver. Once we were practicing with it, the gun suddenly misfired, but luckily, the barrel was pointing towards the ground, and the bullet hit the carpet, penetrating it. We were just engaged and these were the fun things we did as our honeymoon. Later we would explain the hole in the carpet as a memory of our engagement.

The universities were shut down, but Ismail remained in Tehran. He would say, "Although the universities are shut down, the fight is still ongoing." I was worried about him. It was January 1979, and Imam Khomeini had just returned to Iran; a return that was inevitable and nobody could delay it any longer. The television broadcasted it too, but they covered it up with the picture of the Shah quickly. Some people were so angry about this event that they broke their television sets. I called everywhere that I thought might have some news on Ismail's whereabouts, but there was nothing. I considered him my husband and worried about him more than usual. He called on February 12 and gave me the news of the triumph of the revolution and the establishment of a new committee that he was a member of. He said he had been busy with some of his friends trying to move the guns out of the army camps into trucks to stop militia groups from being armed.

The Shah was overthrown, and we were very happy about it, as we considered ourselves as part of its success. Many aspects were yet to become clear with the revolution, which did eventually. One of them was our marriage. We decided to be officially married in 1980 as we had more free time. My mother had asked for a heavy dowry so at least one thing of the marriage that she disapproved of so much could look like a typical marriage of that time. We did not want to accept the condition, but Ismail said, "We have broken your mother's heart with our decisions too many times. What difference does it make to me? Too much or too little, I have nothing to give. Come to think of it; I sometimes wonder what if you asked for your dowry and left me ashamed?!" I told him that I did not want the dowry in the first place, whether they wrote it on our marriage certificate or not.

From the very first days of our marriage, I realized how simple and easy-going Ismail was. He had borrowed some money from someone and had been looking to buy things for us on his own. He had seen a ring in a jewelry store that he liked and wanted to buy. The shopkeeper had handed him the ring and he simply put it in his pocket and paid the price. The shopkeeper had surprised, "Don't you want it for the engagement party?"

"Yes," Ismail replied.

The shopkeeper continued, "You have come here alone, on your own to buy the engagement ring. Now you simply put it in your pocket?! This is not the correct way. You have to gift it to her in a box." He was embarrassed that he had never found the time to learn these customs.

Our marriage ceremony was simple and private. Ismail was wearing a suit; I guess he had borrowed it from his brother. He had been to the barber shop as well. I was wearing a simple shirt with a skirt that one of my friends had made for me and a white veil. We insisted on the simplicity of everything. The engagement table was a simple tablecloth, whereby the most expensive accessory on it was the ring that Ismail had bought for 150 tomans. It was common to give rice and stew for dinner in wedding ceremonies, but Ismail said, "I like *dampokhtak* more." There was nothing fancy at our wedding. We did not even take photographs. Another tradition that we completely broke was bringing a religious lady to give a talk at our wedding instead of music and dancing. She spoke about the positive points regarding marriage. Our wedding ceremony was unlike other ceremonies. Pondering upon it now, I feel we might have been too extreme about our beliefs back then. Nevertheless, nobody could say anything against our will in that matter, and we said the final word on how we wanted the ceremony to take place.

After the ceremony, we returned to Tehran. It felt like we had left something back there. Although we were both university students, there were no universities to attend. The revolution had reached the country's cultural aspect, and all the universities were shut down. Ismail and I would only go to the university without attending any classes to see which party would give a speech that day. Ismail was not my cousin anymore. We had become even more intimate; he was now my husband. When we stayed in Tehran after the ceremony, Ismail worked in the Komite-ye Enqelab Organization and then in Jihad-e Sazandegi Organization. Then, he joined the Islamic Revolutionary Guard Corps (IRGC)[14] through his friendship with Mr. Mohsen Rezaee. The IRGC had turned

---

14. Islamic Revolutionary Guard Corps, or *Sepah*, is a military and cultural organization, which was established about three months after the victory of the Islamic Revolution of Iran (in April 1979) under Imam Khomeini's advisement to protect the revolution and its achievements and to cooperate with the army of the Islamic Republic of Iran.

a confiscated house on Shariati street into a shared living area, and we were granted a room there. We had found what we missed in Tehran again; an excitement from our dull monotonous life. Our life as a couple had started with the revolution, and it was natural to move forward with its tone. The "Komala"[15] party was instigating trouble in the west, and we could hear some action happening from the Iraqi borders as well. Ismail said, "Masoumeh, we need to quit the universities and return to the south."

It was the summer of 1980 that we returned to Aghajari. Mr. Rezayi had ordered Ismail to establish an IRGC branch there. After a long time away from our hometown, we were going back but did not even have a house to live in together.

One of our relatives planned to go on vacation during the summer, and his house would be vacant. He gave us the keys to the house. Ismail had brought a lot of guns from Tehran in order to establish a base in

---

15. The democratic Kurd is a socialist Kurdish party in Western Iran, which demanded for autonomy of the Kurdistan region. To impose its demand, it started armed rebels, and during the Iraqi war on Iran, it fought the Iranian military forces inside Iran.

Aghajari. We hid all of them in the closets at the house. Once the owners returned for a visit, they saw a lot of guns inside their closets instead of clothes for a newlywed couple. They felt really sorry for me, to have to be involved with such things in the early days of my marriage. I told myself, "The bride who started her married life by learning how to use a revolver, of course, was going to live with a musketeer." We spent the whole summer in that house. After the summer, we raised a wall inside Ismail's father's shop and created a room for ourselves. That was our first house. I took my small dowery, and we officially started our married life together there.

My mother used to say, "We allowed our daughter to marry a university student; he turned out to be an IRGC guard." However, the revolution and the war did not make a difference between a student and an IRGC guard. We had grown used to a life like that. It was like going down a path that we started together. Later on, Ismail started looking for new recruits for the IRGC. Although many people volunteered, he was very severe and selective about choosing the right candidates. We later saw the result of his tough interviews and decision-making during the war, as the people he had recruited showed much valor.

Our livelihood was based on the little payment he received from the IRGC and my tutoring money. At least I could do something useful as well by using my community college degree. I had started teaching theology at the only segregated high school for girls in Aghajari. I would teach what I had learned during the revolution to the students.

Chapter 3

Living Next to the Frontline

Only one year had passed when we relocated to Ahvaz because of Ismail's job, another confiscated house that a few other families lived inside as well, located in the Kourosh neighborhood. We had nothing but a 12-meter carpet. However, we established a simple life by borrowing some money from a few friends.

God blessed us with our first child in that house; Ibrahim. He was so proud of having a son and felt really happy about it. Perhaps he was thinking about the future of my life without him and knew how a son could help his lonely mother. Ibrahim always had a grim face. I would tease his father and say, "How come you are always smiling, but your son is always frowning?" His friends would say, "Maybe he wants to become an officer. This is the look of a commander." The arrival of the kid completely changed the nature of our problems. Ibrahim was not a calm and easy kid, and Ismail would spend his time either in the IRGC meetings or somewhere I was oblivious. He would do a lot of suspicious activities as well. Only later, I realized that before the war was officially declared, he and Mohammad Jahanara[16] had engaged the Iraqi troops a few times. Back then, he would not tell me about those matters. I would ask him, "Where do you stay during these nights that you don't even come back home?" He would reply, "I sleep at the IRGC headquarters."

> *She stared at the trees and thought she heard some footsteps approaching. She had told Ismail several times that, "the house is full of guns and it is not safe at home and to come back quickly." But he had yet to come back. It was dark outside, and there was nothing around*

---

16. Seyyed Mohammad Ali Jahanara (1954-1981) was the commander of Khorramshahr branch of Islamic Revolutionary Guard Corp during the Iraqi war on Iran. He played a key role in freeing Khorramshahr and breaking the siege of Abadan.

the house but wilderness. She picked up the handgun Ismail had given her for such situations. She stared into the darkness and yelled, "Stop," but nobody responded. She knew there was something out there, and could hear the heavy footsteps of a guy approaching on the leaves on the ground. She thought there were at least a few men. She could hear each one's footsteps as they were approaching. The gun was cold and her hands were sweaty. They were still moving forward. She thought to herself: "What if they cut off my head...." She pictured it and it made her more stressed. She yelled: "Stop!" again and thought, "Well, it is obvious they know there is a woman all alone in the house." She checked the gun; the safety was off. She pointed the gun towards the sound and waited. The shadows were out of the trees. Looking at the scene, she did not know whether she should laugh or start cursing. There was a herd of cows looking at her for a while. There were four or five of them. The one leading the herd kept on its way, and the rest of the herd followed it into the trees.

On the morning of September 4, 1980,

I was awoken by the loud sound of an explosion. The sound was the start of a conflict. The Iraqi fighter jets had broken through the sonic barrier. When Ismail returned home at night, I asked him, "What was that sound?" He replied, "Saddam[17] decided to pay us a visit." He knew a war was going to break out sooner or later, but did not tell us anything about it. He kept his secrecy to the end and would talk less about the matters of war at home. Two weeks later, the war officially broke out. Saddam thought he could take the Khuzestan province in a week. Most people evacuated the city, but we stayed put.

One day he came and told me, "Create a foxhole in the yard." I asked, "You think I can do it?" He said, "Yes. If you work at it every day, it will finish soon." I used a shovel to build a small trench in the yard,

---

17. Saddam Hussein (1937-2006) was a military general and the leader of the Ba'ath party in Iraq. From 1979 to 2003, he became the Iraqi president. During his reign, he attacked Iran, the Iraqi Kurdistan, and Kuwait.
For Iranian people, Saddam is recognized as the most bloodthirsty leader in the contemporary world, after the leaders of the Zionist regime and the US.

so Ibrahim and I could take cover when we heard the fighter jets approach. Ibrahim was only two months old and he would cry a lot, from dusk to dawn. When I took him to a doctor, he simply said, "Some children are like this." During the day, I would hear the sound of the missiles and explosions, and during the night Ibrahim's cry. Another problem was that I could not feed him with just my milk, as it was not enough and all the stores were closed.

Our families protested and said, "What have these poor souls done to deserve to stay with you under all these missiles and artillery fire?!" Ismail replied, "It is not right for my family and child to be far away from the war and its dangers while I have so many responsibilities related to it."

Saddam had miscalculated. The Khuzestan province did not surrender in a week. With the start of the war, the rest of our life was mapped out for us. Ismail accepted different responsibilities that would lead him to the front lines one way or another. The whole Khuzestan province was the area of his operations and he had to travel all the time. If he stayed at home for at least two nights a week, it meant that he was being generous towards me.

One night Ismail was supposed to put Ibrahim to sleep to understand how difficult things were without him. I told him, "Now see which one is harder, putting your kid to sleep or fighting a war?" He replied, "Of course, fighting a war." The following day, he said, "The Iraqi soldiers would go silent when you fire a bullet at them, whereas this kid simply does not care. I used all my stories, lullabies and techniques, but he just did not budge."

One time Ismail got back late at night, and hungry from a work trip after several days. We had nothing to eat at home. We sat down and ate all the bread leftovers from weeks ago. Eventually, he realized when he was not around, things were not okay at all. As we only met once a month, it was better for us to be somewhere safer as Ahvaz had turned into the frontline for the whole conflict.

We moved to Qom[18] in 1981. Ibrahim was just 11 months old. Ismail said, "You

---

18. Qom is the second most important pilgrimage city in Iran, where the mausoleum of Lady Masumah (a), the daughter of Imam al-Kazim (a) and the sister of Imam al-Ridha (a) is located. The city has always been home to Shiite scholars and authorities.

won't feel bored without me here in Qom anymore." He left us there and disappeared. We were staying at a relative's house. Ibrahim needed full time attention and had his own naughty games. We caused our poor relatives so much trouble until he returned to rent a house.

We rented a house from one of his cleric friends. He and his wife lived in the same building. For my convenience, they left to live upstairs and allowed me to live on the ground floor. My sister and her kid accompanied me from Aghajari so we would not feel lonely. Luckily, we did not have too much furniture, so we could easily relocate quickly and adapt to living in a new house. We had bought a secondhand fridge that made a lot of noise and a small oven. The most serious difficulty we had back then was buying a gas capsule. I made Ismail promise to help me with the replacement of the gas capsule and take responsibility for it. It only took him a few days until he completely forgot about his promise. He just left and said, "I will be back before this capsule finishes." I suppose it was Operation Beit ol-Moqaddas. We finished two more capsules but he did not show up. After his return, we went to Mashhad[19] to attend a seminar intended for IRGC commanders. It was a memorable trip for us both, since neither of us had been to Mashhad before. It was not deemed bad, but he felt a bit embarrassed to leave his colleagues and sit beside me on the bus. The basement of a mosque was turned into a hotel for the attendees, but it was the same story at the hotel as well. He was off again to tend to his work affairs. I was finally able to persuade him to go to the holy shrine one night together. What I wanted to ask Imam Reza to grant me was for the two of them, father and son, to come to their senses a little bit. Perhaps Ibrahim would cry less and Ismail would stay at home a bit longer.

Ismail felt satisfied with such a lifestyle; the fact that our life was not dragged down by a monotonous daily routine and all our concerns were not shifted towards materialistic goals, like adding more furniture to the house. He had turned me into a person just like himself. I would try to buy the simplest clothes; and the cheapest. It was not a matter of affordability. Each

---

19. Mashhad is a city in northeastern Iran, located in the center of Razavi Khorasan Province. The city is home to the mausoleum of Imam al-Ridha (a), the eighth Shiite Imam.

month that he got his payment from the IRGC he would use some of it to pay for work trips and leave the remainder for me. However, I did not have any demands for unimportant and materialistic life matters either. I believed with his presence, the materialistic needs were really shallow and unnecessary. Women are known for being interested in jewelry and other beautiful things, but I never thought about buying particular accessories or any special clothes. He would say, "Masoumeh, you are such a winner in these matters." I would ask, "What do you mean?" He would reply, "You are not obsessed with unimportant matters. Be happy about it. He kept saying, "Let's leave thinking about an easy life for after the war."

I would never consider his lack of presence on account of indifference to his wife and family. I had grown used to a life like that with him. I got this feeling with him that I was living for a higher purpose.

I remember he fell asleep on one of his trips to which I was accompanying him. He pulled over the car, took off his boots, and put them outside since there was not enough space in the car. After taking a nap, we got back on the road again. Only thirty minutes had passed that he realized he had left his boots on the ground. He quickly calculated the price of a pair of new boots. He also considered the price of the gas and car depreciation if we were to go back and pick them up. The price of the boots was higher so we turned back. Luckily, the pair of boots were still on the ground next to the road.

I was lucky for a few days to have him beside me after a long period of time and distance between us. In 1982 or 1983, he started studying again, as the war had gone softer and the top generals had decided to keep him away from the frontlines. He was assigned as the head of "the Intelligence Protection Organization of the Islamic Revolutionary Guards Corps" in Qom and Markazi provinces. Back then, there were too many assassinations carried out by the "Munafiqin Organization."[20] He was in charge of protecting the religious scholars

---

20. People's Mujahedin Organization (MEK), known in Iran as Munafiqin (Hypocrites), is a scandalous terrorist group that fled Iran in 1981, because of its conflicts with the religious beliefs of the Iranian people and the government, resulting in widespread assassinations and slaughters of the Iranian people and the officials of the Islamic Republic of Iran.

and Ayatollahs. It was an opportunity for him to learn about the seminary. That year was the only time in our marriage that our life was somewhat normal. Like a normal person, he would go to work in the morning and return home in the evening. After a while, the routine changed to staying at home in the mornings as well, and just going to work in the afternoon. I made a joke and said, "You seem like people with no jobs that stay at home all the time." He replied, "Now that I have accepted to stay at home, you don't want me to?!" He said, "I stay at home in the mornings to study the lessons for the starter level of the seminary. Then I go to the office in the afternoon. You know I cannot sit behind a desk for too long." He put his books in the corner of the room, bought a small table and started studying.

We did not have enough money to buy a telephone. The IRGC wanted to establish a telephone line for our house from the office, but he did not accept it. His excuse was, "It would interrupt my studies." He really had committed himself to studying. He had a notebook to do the English and Arabic language assignments as well. When he stayed at home for more than a few days in the morning, I asked, "Can't you simply find a job to work in the mornings?!" I was not used to seeing him at home so much.

She remembered their old house. Ismail had constructed a small treehouse with pieces of wood and iron as a hiding spot for the kids. He would invite everyone to come and visit his small house. Nobody would dare to go up the high ladder. One day he had decided to take her to the treehouse to show her his private and secretive lounge. Later he explained the reason for only helping her, "Because you were the most innocent kid." He had trusted her since they were children and nothing had changed since then. She believed his words from the day she accepted his proposal. She knew it with all her heart, as she had lost all her emotions and thirst for love into the depth of the unending ocean in his eyes. A man who would leave by his own will, but would only return by God's will. With the war going on, she did not expect her life to be normal and peaceful anymore. There were so many secrets in such tiny houses. Living her life beside him with all its difficulties gave her a sort of excitement that she could not simply find in living

with any ordinary man.

Over that one year, I got a sample of how sweet life could be beside him with a lot of patience—living an ordinary life. It was the only year in the period of our marriage that the neighbors were able to see a person who would normally come and go as my husband. In the previous houses that we lived in, he either did not come home at all or would come so late and leave so soon that nobody would be able to see him. After he was martyred, they realized who the man who would come to the mosque at midnight and wash the dishes leftover from the dinner actually was. He would work without any expectations of recognition. For example, his position at the IRGC that none of the neighbors really knew about. I was pregnant with our second child Zahra, during the time that he was at home studying. I still remember the yard in that small house in Qom. There was a pomegranate tree in its middle, and you could hear the beautiful, heartwarming sound of Quran recitation on the radio early in the mornings. During the holy month of Ramadan, he would read through the whole of the Holy Quran at least once. He would read the Quran with a nice tone and a correct manner. He would put

Ibrahim on his lap, and our son would move his head, imitating his dad's movement, as if he were reading the Quran too. He also took Ibrahim to Friday prayers[21]. Every other week we would go on a picnic, though. He would say, "We should go to the arms of mother nature."

His youthful energy did not decrease with marriage or age; he would play soccer, go swimming and mountain climbing. I taught him chess and he would checkmate us all.

---

21. Friday prayer consists of two units (*rak'ahs*), which is performed in a certain way at noon on Friday. In particular, before performing the prayer, the imam of Friday prayer delivers a sermon to the worshipers, which includes themes such as the call to God-wariness as well as political and social issues pertaining to Muslims.

Chapter 4

A Commander Only Outside the House

Back then, Mr. Mazaheri[22] conducted a few lectures for the IRGC commanders on how to treat their wives at home. Once, he came home laughing. I asked him, "What's the matter?" He replied, "Mr. Mazaheri has taught us something that we are not allowed to share with women. But I cannot simply keep it a secret." I asked him why and he said, "Because you are different from all other women." I said, "What do you mean?" He said, "I have been away from you for so

---

22. Ayatollah Hossein Mazaheri (b. 1933) is a Shiite authority and the head of the seminary of Isfahan. He had lectures on ethics for decades, and published Islamic ethical works such as a book on struggle against the self (*jihad al-nafs*).

long that it feels like we are more like friends than just husband and wife." I questioned, "Are you going to tell me or what?" He said, "Mr. Mazaheri has strongly advised us to confess our feelings and love to our wives." They had made a bet on who would have the courage to go and confess his love to his wife and tell her that he loved her. I said, "Thank God, somebody finally taught you guys something about these matters." Even if he did not say it, I still knew it, though.

Once we did not look eye to eye on a matter. Each one of us insisted on our point of view. However, in the end he became angry. He always had a happy face, but this time he had a grim look on his face and had a strict tone in his voice. He left the house and returned home with the same smile as usual. He would say, "We should not allow our fights and disagreements to last for more than a day."

It was the year 1981 when my brother was martyred. I became really sad in my heart. There was not much of an age gap between us, and I loved him so dearly. I did not kiss him goodbye so he had to return to us but he did not. My mother had asked Ismail to at least stop him from going to the frontlines if he could not prevent him from joining the ranks. My brother was young and had a sort of calm and peaceful manner. My mother was gifted with him after having six daughters and resorting to prayers and vows to God for so long. Ismail would say: "Why did he have to go and I...." He would return from all the operations in one piece and did not talk about martyrdom during the course of our married life. He would not say that he was going to be a martyr at all. Even if he talked about the war and frontlines, it would be about the success and progress of our troops. He would not talk about the difficulties and the stress of the battles. That made me think that we were successful in all the operations.

Ismail grew tired of having a desk job after just one year. He told Mr. Mohsen Rezaee that he could not handle nor want an office responsibility anymore. He wrote a letter saying, "With the amount of information I have about the warzone and frontlines, I can no longer stay in this office. I can be of more use there. If you do not accept this, I will simply resign and join the frontlines as a simple '*basiji*'[23] volunteer." It was the same

---

23. In Iran, *basiji* refers to every person who tries to protect the Islamic Republic and defend the ideals

time that Imam had said, "The war is the country's top priority and above everything else." What Imam said was like a textbook guideline to him; he would write them down and memorize them. Mr. Rezaee assigned him to be in charge of the Malik Ashtar project; a training course designed for IRGC high-ranking commanders to become more familiar with classical warfare tactics. They would provide the commanders with some scores and in the end some certification as well. Life was back to normal; he would come home late, and I would still wait for him. After the martyrdom of my brother, there was no joy left in our family. Not only was I pregnant, but also had to give my family some comfort as well. I stayed in Aghajari with my mother so she could feel better. There was a celebration at the mosque on the 13th day of the month of Rajab.[24] Ibrahim and I attended it and had as much "*Zoolbia*"[25] as we could. On the way

---

of its founder, Imam Khomeini, even if they are not official members of the *Basij* organization.

24. The Thirteenth day of the seventh lunar month (Rajab) is the birth anniversary of Imam Ali (a), the first Shiite Imam. Shias celebrate this day worldwide. Since the 1979 Islamic Revolution, this day has been marked as Father's Day, in Iran.

25. Jalebi (Persian: *zoolbia*) is a kind of confection,

back home from the mosque, I felt a pain in my stomach and that was how we had our second child Zahra before the *adhan* of the morning prayers of the 13th of Rajab. Ismail was stationed in the West back then. He made it back as soon as possible to recite the *adhan* in our child's ears himself. Zahra's birth made him super happy. He was excited about the whole situation. He would say, "A girl gets special respect and treatment in the family." and would caress her all the time. He liked her so much that I got worried that Ibrahim might become jealous.

I had grown tired of being a housewife. I sensed that my life had become entirely monotonous. I felt like I needed to become a student again. I told him, "If you recall, I was not a housewife when we got married; I was a university student. Now I want to go back to university and get the degree I left unfinished." He responded, "It's up to you to do as you please." At one point, he wanted to continue his education, but when he gave it a second thought, he realized he could not stay put in one place anymore. The last time he studied something as a student was five

---

which is commonly served in Iran during the month of Ramadhan when breaking the fast.

years before that.

Returning to the faculty was not an easy job. The old employees when they saw me would say, "Eh… You are still alive?!" After some struggle, they allowed me to continue my education. I returned to Tehran, this time with two children. One of the dormitories was dedicated to married women, and we could take our children and stay there alongside some other single students. I moved in with my children. Once again, I was going back to the lively days of university. At first, I was not doing so good, but after a semester I was back on track.

I recall that I had to get up very early in the morning to take the children to school and kindergarten. Ibrahim was too old for kindergarten and I needed to take him to an elementary school. Then I had to rush to reach my morning classes. I was the only girl in the class. Everybody would say, "Why do you need to study with two children and a soldier as a husband?" But Ismail, who could see how the classes had affected me and my spirit, was very supportive of my decision. It was as if we liked to put ourselves into hardship. During this period, I would see Ismail more as a friend; a friend whom I would just see every once in a while. He would leave his bag at the dormitory and go to do some shopping for me and take the children out when he visited.

I was supposed to study just to get my associate degree, but since I liked studying so much, I asked for Ismail's opinion about my options. I said, "Do you want me to quit so I can pay more attention to the children?" He did not accept it. He said, "No, you should not give up on this. If you give up on your passion, you will allow yourself to give up on something later for our children as well."

He was happy that I had an interest in continuing with my education. He said, "Well, I am just getting started with the more serious missions on the front lines. You can even stay here and attain your master's degree if you wish."

Ibrahim was getting older, and it was not right to stay at that dormitory with all the girls anymore. Ismail's friends found an apartment for us with low rent. They were not easy days. Studying and taking care of children – especially Ibrahim whom I was sure had taken after his father because he was a very stubborn child. Tehran's missile barrage and his absence for a few months made it even harder. To make matters even worse, he took all sorts of missions on the front lines. Thinking back, I realized I could see him more often when we were not married.

It was the year 1984 and the war had reached its critical point. He created a new branch on the front lines; the Badr brigade composed of Iraqi fighters and civilians, who had decided to take up arms against Saddam's "*Ba'thi*" invaders for the sake of Islam. One day when he became ill and was resting at home, a few people came to visit him with fruits and sweets. After catering for them as our guests, when they left, he said, "Would you promise not to get angry if I told you who they were?" I said, "Of course not, how come?!" He said, "They were Iraqi soldiers." The *Ba'thi* soldiers had martyred my brother, and my brother-in-law was a POW. Regardless of all the pain they had caused us, he explained the situation to me. They made the right choice for that position. I knew nobody could be as kind as Ismail when he decided to be kind. During the one and half years that he was in charge of the Badr brigade, he had become like one of them, as if they were part of his family. He felt worried and responsible for every single one of them. He would say, "These people have nobody but us in this country and are our guests." He took care of everything for them, visited their homes and even cared for times when they ran out of things like cigarettes. He had studied educational sciences and was a good advisor to them. He found one of them a decent girl to marry as well. The Iraqi man would say, "Mr. Ismail was the first person who gave me a feeling of security in Iran."

At first, I wondered how he could work with the people whose language he did not understand. Only later I realized he could speak Arabic as fluently as a native. He would call me in front of them "Umm Ibrahim" and participate in their religious events and recite the Supplication of Kumayl[26] in an Arabic accent for them. Some of them only realized he was not an Arab after his martyrdom. They would say, "He is the second Imam Musa al-Sadr[27] to us". In the

---

26. The supplication of Kumayl is a mystical supplication, which Imam Ali (a) taught Kumayl b. Ziyad, a close companion of him. It is commonly recited by Shias, particular on Thursday nights.
27. Sayyid Musa al-Sadr (b. 1928), known as Imam Musa al-Sadr, was a Shiite leader in Lebanon and a founder of the Supreme Islamic Shia Council

Badr brigade, Ismail did an exceptional job. Some Iraqi soldiers were captured in one operation and fought against their regime in the next operation.

9th Badr brigade was the first official Iraqi military movement after establishing the Islamic Supreme council of Iraq[28] against Saddam's regime—a dictator who had become in charge through force and manipulation. With Iraqi militia and freedom fighters as its initial core, they felt the need for military actions against Saddam. Prior to that, there had been several talks amongst Iranian leaders, militia and freedom fighters for the need of such an organization, but it seemed something was not right. The two parties could not understand and trust each other completely. Ismail Daqayeqi was assigned as the head of the project to bring the leaders of the Iraqi freedom fighters

---

in Lebanon and Amal Movement (a major Shia institution in Lebanon). He struggled for the coexistence of religions, proximity between Islamic denominations, and liberation of Palestinians.
28. The Islamic Supreme Council of Iraq or the Supreme Council for the Islamic Revolution in Iraq is an Islamist party for Iraqi Shias, established in 1982 by Iran-based dissident Iraqi clerics to fight against Saddam's regime.

together, who were all unknown individuals away from each other in different cities. He was assigned to organize the whole battalion, a task that could benefit Iranians in several aspects if carried out successfully. After so many sessions with the head of the government and many hours of negotiations, he was able to get their approval. He was in charge of the negotiations and organization of the Iraqi side as well. He had to get to know every one of them at a deeper level in order to trust them. He would travel to several locations and talk to so many people to get them to join each other. The Islamic Revolutionary fighters and the Iraqis who had run away in fear of Saddam's aggression and oppression were scattered in different locations. They were all from different tribes, with different accents and cultures.

Possessing mere commanding skills was not enough to rally them to fight beside the Iranian soldiers against their own countrymen. The scene where he was sitting beside an old Iraqi gypsy to see whether he had sugar in his house for tea was not just a show for modesty. He knew it well that leading through people's hearts would last forever and was much safer. Later, when the intelligence office wanted to erect some barbed wires around the *Tawwab*[29] POW camp, he refused. He said, "I personally take the responsibility for all the Iraqi captives in this camp." To deliver on his promise, he paid less attention to his wife and children. With all his efforts, the Badr battalion was turned into a brigade and later into an army division. At first, they were only assigned to reconnaissance missions, but later they turned into an operational division.

Once, he had seen a young Iraqi soldier who was well equipped. However, he realized he was not authorized to carry any grenades when he inspected him carefully. He was offended. He personally went to the supply depot and brought him a grenade. Many did not even know the guy who cleaned his own cabin every morning, joined them for performing the daily prayers, paid attention to drink his tea with sugar not sugar cubes, spoke Arabic fluently and called everyone "*akhi*"(my brother), was in fact their commanding officer. Later, they saw the same guy in an operation that tried

---

29. Repentant Iraqi prisoners of war are those Iraqi prisoners who gave up the fight against Iran when they were taken to Iran, saw the treatment by Iranians, as well as the real face of the Islamic Republic and the Iranian people.

to save a fellow soldier on the other side of the frontlines, who was being captured and brought him back over to the friendly lines.

I was worried about the children, because they did not see their father as often as a normal kid did. My concern was that he might become a stranger to them. When I was staying at the dormitory, no man was allowed inside. Later, when we moved out of the dormitory, he did not find the time to visit. One day, when he wanted to go to the frontlines, he hugged Zahra, kissed her goodbye, and said, "Goodbye, sweetheart." Zahra responded in her own cute words, "No Goodbye." We all started crying. His mother who was staying over at our place that day, insisted on him to delay his departure for at least one day. He said, "I love this child more than any of you, but my love and commitment to God's command is much more." Zahra was a girl, and her feelings were closer to mine. I told him, "Shouldn't this boy get a chance to spend some time with his father?" He said, "I have no other place but the frontlines to take him." I insisted on him to take Ibrahim the next time that he wanted to leave. Ibrahim was only six years old, loved guns and ammunitions and really wanted to go with his father. Ismail took him on one of his tours which lasted for about a month; they went to the opening ceremonies of a few training camps in Bakhtaran.[30] He still remembers some of the good memories of those days.

> *The kid woke up, a bit late of course. And during that time, all the soldiers, who were exhausted and hungry, had eaten all the food. Walking for hours in the mountains had completely drained all of their energy. When the kid woke up, he looked around and said, "Daddy, I want some eggs as well." But the eggs were finished, and he would not accept anything else but eggs. Ibrahim was insistent on wanting eggs. "I want eggs for breakfast," he said. The men looked at each other. There was simply no solution. Two hours later, a soldier approached, breathing heavily with a few eggs in his hands. The whole war was like a game to the child that only tough men around him with grim faces could understand. He devoured*

---

30. Bakhtaran is the previous name of Kermanshah and an ancient city in Iran. During the Iraqi *Ba'ath* regime's war on Iran, the city was frequently under air and ground attacks by the Iraqi army.

his breakfast clueless of all the trouble and difficulty the poor soldier had been through to bring him a few eggs. A while later, he fell asleep again.

During the ten months that we had moved out of the dormitory to the house on Shariati Street, he only visited us twice; once when visiting Ayatollah Hakim and discussing an issue with him, and another time to rest at home as he was sick. He had gotten the flu and had an infection in his throat and chest. In order to trick him into staying a bit longer, I said, "It's probably tuberculosis." It worked and I was able to keep him at home for a few days longer. I was used to not seeing him, though. Based on the laws in the battlefield, he could return home for 15 days after staying in the frontlines for 45 days. But he did not use that right. The kids, just like me, considered seeing their father as a wish that was granted every once in a blue moon. They loved him so much, because he favored and protected them all the time. I could not yell at them in front of him because it made him angry. I could not take the children with me out for shopping when he was around, as he would say, "They will get tired." His friends called him "the temperamental Ismail" for his unique method of educating his children. He would say, "A kid should grow based on his or her humane temperament. We should not force anything against their will." Every time that he returned, the children's commotion seemed very sweet to him. Even if they were minding their own business and were too quiet, he would do something to make them make a noise. He would imitate animals for them, like making the sound of a sheep. They enjoyed it very much as well. He was only a commander outside the house. He would never force his opinion onto me. If he did not agree with something, he would say, "Listen Masoumeh, I cannot accept what you are saying but that does not mean I do not care for you." During our married life, he raised his voice at me only once. His mother talked me into leaving the house and staying away from the warzone for a while, so I left Ahvaz and went to Aghajari to feel safer. He came right after me. He raised his voice in front of his friends at the door, "Why aren't you getting in the car?" He quickly realized that he had not acted appropriately. He drove off for a while and returned again, but this time, he convinced me to go back with him. Once when we were talking about our memories, he told me, "Masoumeh I have not done right by you this whole time."

I said, "We haven't spent that much time together as a couple for you to say that. It has always been me on my own." He said, "I am talking about the time you were in Ahvaz. I took you there so I would not feel lonely. Some nights, you were hungry without me even being around."

One day, the kids were sitting in front of him and playing. Ibrahim bothered Zahra a little and made her cry. Ismail loved Zahra so much, and in order to teach Ibrahim a lesson, he slapped him softly. Later he realized he had acted out of anger and asked for Ibrahim's forgiveness. That night I realized that sleep was eluding him. He was busy with something, so I pretended that I was asleep. At midnight I saw him praying. I had not seen him pray in the middle of the night. He did such actions in a way that everything seemed normal, and nobody could notice them. After finishing up his prayers, he went to Ibrahim's bedside and cried.

She was getting to know him little by little. They had about five years of memories together. She knew it well they were not fake. He was not pretending. And he knew well how different the frontlines and home should

be; how to treat his wife and children. And what she had asked God was for their lives not to be monotonous. Only if... No, she did not want to have any objections. Her father had put it well, "Ismail does not belong to this world," he had said, "He was lucky that there was a war going on."

Once Ismail told me, "There is a program in 'Dezful'[31] tomorrow for the soldiers' wives. Go there and give a speech," he said. I questioned, "What? I go and give them a speech? But I ..." He said, "There is nothing to it."

The following day, when she saw the crowd of women waiting for her to give them a speech, she felt really stressed. she had not spoken in front of a crowd before. When she began to speak, her voice was shaking at first. she talked about her life and the ups and downs of living with an IRGC member. she talked about the fact that if she wanted it, she could have an easy and normal

---

31. Dezful is a city in southwestern Iran in Khuzestan Province. During the Iraqi war on Iran, the city came under 160 missile attacks, and nearly 2600 people in the city were martyred.

life like other wives; attending different parties and hosting some parties herself as well. But she did not want that. Because at that very moment, many people were being slaughtered under the fires of war and it was not the right thing to do. When she finished her talk, she felt a heavy burden lifted off her chest. she did not consider what she told them as a speech, it was more like opening up to some people who were just like her. The crowd was silent and listening to her words. she had not lied or over-exaggerated anything; she had only shared the story of her life.

One day when Ismail had returned, I told him: "I don't have the heart to visit my friend whose husband has been martyred on the front lines." He asked: "Why? What's wrong with it? You know there is a chance for me to get martyred in the coming months, and you will be the widow of shaheed Daqayeqi." I was not used to him talking like that; talking about martyrdom. "Only the worthy are the chosen martyrs and once God sees your worth, you have to answer the call."

Chapter 5

Ahvaz, Our Last Reunion

The last time we saw each other in our house in Tehran was the November of 1986. There was still one month left until his departure but how could I have known? He returned from the front lines, bought a doll for Zahra and a tricycle for Ibrahim. When we were saying goodbye, he said, "Don't you want a lift?" I was shocked because he was sensitive about using the office car and equipment for personal use. We had never used any IRGC cars to go anywhere for a personal purpose together. I said, "Well about time!" He said, "I am headed to the direction of the university for a work-related task. And I am not wearing the IRGC uniform. So..." He gave me a lift to the university and left.

A few weeks before leaving me alone on this earth, he called and said, "Come to Ahvaz." I said, "I am in the middle of my midterm exams. I am a bit busy and the kids have to go to school." He said, "Well, try to make it work if possible, please." Our relationship was very close and friendly, so we could tell each other how we felt. He called a few more times. I said, "You come!" He said, "I am caught up at work and cannot leave." He called one more time but I told, "If I come now, I will fall behind for one semester." He continued, "It's different this time," he said reassuringly. "What is the difference? Perhaps you have fallen in love, huh?" I asked. "What's wrong with a man being in love with his wife?" He questioned. "Do come. You will regret it later because we might not see each other for a few months at all," he said.

I was shocked. Every time that he wanted to see us, he would visit himself. I thought, what if he was injured and not able to come to Tehran. Operation Karbala-5[32] was

---

32. Operation Karbala-5 is an operation carried out by Armed Forces of Iran during the Iraqi war on Iran to conquer Basra. Although Iranians could not conquer Basra in that operation, they successfully freed Shalamcheh and took control of parts of southern

about to start. But he was not like that. He would always say, "You have gotten used to my absence like all other IRGC members' families." And now he was insisting on us meeting him in the south. I realized it must be a serious situation.

I had a strange dream during that period. It looked like there was going to be an operation of some sorts. The soldiers were getting on a train. I was standing in the middle of the crowd bidding the fighters, amongst whom was Ismail, farewell. Ismail separated himself from the line and called me up to the platform. The platform was filled with a lot of people. I went up. He approached to say goodbye. I felt a bit shy in the crowd, but it seemed the others could not see us. He pulled me into his arms and held me tight. He kept me in his arms, and we both started crying. When I woke up from my sleep, my eyes were still wet with tears.

Throughout all those years, he had only phoned a few times; a couple of times on our neighbor's line in Qom (as we did not have a telephone in our own house) and a

---

Iraq. It was the most costly and the deadliest Iranian operation during the Iraqi war on Iran.

couple of times when I was at the dormitory in Tehran. It was a bit odd to ask me to go to the south, while we usually would not get any news from him for a couple of months straight. Finally, I accepted it, but under one condition, I told him, "If I come there, we have to be together for at least one week. You are not allowed to go anywhere to take care of any side missions. "I accept," he said. He had made the preparations beforehand with his friends. He called them and said, "Masoumeh has agreed to come, go and pick her up."

We got on the road in an IRGC car. When we got closer to Khuzestan province, I realized although my husband was a fighter in the IRGC army, I did not have a realistic understanding on how severe the conditions were in the south. We had to stop the car in a few spots and take cover beside the road. The Iraqis were bombarding the area with missiles. We got to Ahvaz at the time of morning prayers before dawn. I saw Ismail in front of the door waiting for us. He picked up the children who were sleeping in the car and took them inside the house.

I had cooked his favorite meal in Tehran; rice and yogurt. He had the food for breakfast. In less than an hour he said,

"Well I have to go now." I told him, "You dragged us all the way down here to tell us that you are leaving?" "Well, you have brought us luck. The operation has moved forward, and it will commence tomorrow night, and I have to be there tonight," he said. I was furious and about to explode. I told him with tears in my eyes, "I will never forgive you if you go to the frontlines today and sleep there for the night," He said, "You were never so cruel. You have a big heart, and these words do not suit your personality. I will come to your sister's house for dinner. I cannot promise you that I will stay for the night, but I will come to say goodbye." I sarcastically responded, "That's really nice of you."

The first time that I really got worried was that time. Never before did I think there was a chance that I would not see him again. We left his friend's house to my sister's place. She was surprised when she saw me. "What are you doing here?" she said. "My husband has fallen in love, so he sent for me," I said. My sister was more furious than I was. She could understand how I felt and how much I needed him to be by my side, just for one night at least. "Don't be sad. He will show up at night. I will make some dinner and once he comes home, we will make him stay one way or another," she said reassuringly. Her prediction was correct. At midnight I heard the doorbell and realized that Ismail was back. When he said goodbye to the driver at the door, I became really excited and happy. I realized he was going to stay for the night. He was wearing his uniform. They were making the preparation for an attack, but his friends had not allowed him to stay. They had told him, "We are ashamed before your wife and kids," and had forced him to return home.

Everyone had a good time that night. After ages, the four of us were together as a family. Ismail was happy and in a good mood. He was making jokes and made everybody laugh. He never was a bore but that night when I paid closer attention, he seemed more content and there was a spark in his eyes. Ibrahim approached him and asked, "Father, what does it mean when you say, There is not much distance to Karbala? How far is Karbala from here anyways?" Ismail showed him the location of Karbala on the map. "Look, this is Ahvaz. This is Abadan. And here is Karbala. Palestine is here as well. It's only a few centimeters away." He said. "You are not telling the truth. It's just on the map like that." Ibrahim responded. "It turns out they have been teaching you a few things at school," Ismail replied.

At night when we were about to go to bed, I realized why I had traveled all that distance; why I had accepted to fail all my lessons. I had the feeling one gets when somebody is going on a long journey and you need to say goodbye to them. "Now that we are all here, please pray to God that a missile hits this house, so we can depart this earth all together, not just you," I told him.

"After all this time fighting and going to the frontlines, is it fair people say that he was martyred beside his wife at home?" he said. He continued, "I pray to God to let whatever that is best for us to happen." He did not say anything about martyrdom, so I would not get suspicious. But one gets a feeling about such things when they are about to happen.

He asked my sister to give him an alarm clock so he could wake up early in the morning. He woke up before dawn and performed his morning prayers. The driver had come to take him. "At least wait for the children to get up to see you and then leave,"

I said, but there was no time left; not even for breakfast. My sister rushed and made some eggs so he could eat on the way. He said, "What about my friends in the car?" We made some more for them as well. I went to accompany him to the door. When he reached the alleyway, he turned back and waved goodbye. He never used to do that.

> *He was standing at the end of the alleyway and waving his hand, fading away with a smile on his face. She wanted to run after him, but it felt like her feet were glued to the ground. She could only watch him go further and further, fading in the distance; like water turning into steam under the sunlight. She wanted to stop him from disappearing into the thin air. She did not want to live with just a memory. After saying goodbye, he did not owe anything to this world. Five hours later, he was at the front lines. The operation details were given to the division. Everybody knew he was going on a reconnaissance mission, as he never felt comfortable sending one of his crew members to a location until he had inspected it himself. Both of them mounted a motorcycle and left together.*

The enemy aircraft was in the area and the motorcycle was a good target. They got off to draw less attention, but the aircraft had already spotted them. The cluster bombs exploded on top of the trenches they had taken shelter in. His brother in arms looked at Ismail to see if he was okay. He was doing well. He had never been any better; lying silently on the ground without uttering a word. A faded smile was on his lips as if he had departed for thousands of years.

Nobody gave the news to the division. On the radio, they kept mentioning his name, so the troops would not lose courage. However, the Ba'athies had happily spread the news already.

I left my sister's house and went to Aghajari to visit my family; it had been a while since I saw them. I had butterflies in my stomach so I could not stay in my mother's house either. I wanted to stay away from my family to feel less stressed and so I decided to pay a visit to the wife of the shaheed Alidadi. He was the same guy who helped Ismail on the day the revolution was successful, to secure all the guns from the army camps. He had just been martyred on Operation Karbala-4. Operation Karbala-4 was really special to me, because later I heard that Ismail took his first ablution (*ghusl*) for martyrdom there. When they asked, "What is the reason for taking an ablution for martyrdom?" He had responded, "Why can't you see that I might have a chance to join the chosen ones? If there is a hidden reason, it would apply to all of us." He later personally delivered the speech at Alidadi's memorial service. Anyway, I went to the house of Mr. Alidadi to see his wife. She asked how Ismail was doing? I said, "There is an operation. He is supposed to come back tomorrow." She joked and said, "Don't worry. The commanders don't easily get martyred, as they don't go to the front lines." I kind of got offended. When I went back home, it was the same night of the operation. I had a weird dream. A big crowd of women were standing in a desert and performing ablution at a small water pool to get ready and perform their prayers. I knew all of them. Mr. Alidadi's wife was there too. I was waiting in line for my turn to go and perform ablution. I asked her, "Are you finished?" she said, "Yes. Soon it will be your turn as well." I said, "Yes. I am almost there."

When I got up in the morning, I was still stuck in the dream I had the night before when the doorbell rang. They said there was a meeting at the mosque with the board of the trustees and my father had to be there. He quickly got dressed and left. Thirty minutes later, when they returned, they said, "Ismail's father is not feeling well, and you should come." Right then, I knew what it was all about. If I had any doubts until then, I was sure after that point. I realized all the news about his father's condition was all a show as his father was completely healthy and well. I realized just like the dream I had the night before, it was my turn. I tried to stay calm. I did not want my mother who was completely crushed over losing my brother, to go through the whole experience again. I went outside and sat in the car. When she saw how calm I was, she felt better. I saw all the neighbors looking at me; as if they knew something was not right. There was not much distance between our house and Ismail's family's; only a few minutes. I saw the placards right at the beginning of the alleyway. Could it be intended for somebody else? No! It was for him. I tried to keep silent; no tears and no emotional reactions. I was like a person who did not have anything else to say once she got the truth. I sat there shocked and confused for about an hour. When I gained control, I asked his friends,

"Before anything else, tell me whether or not there is a body." They assured me that we would get his body, which made me feel better.

To continue my life without knowing what he expected me to do or how he wanted me after that point was difficult. Three years before that, I saw him write something on a piece of paper and put the handwriting between the pages of the Holy Quran, and asked me not to read it. His friends looked for his will and found it in his bag. Before reading it, I checked the date; it was from three years ago. He had written it on the day that lady Fatemeh Al-Zahra[33] (a) was martyred. His martyrdom also happened during the Days of *Fatimiyyah*.[34] After advising us to be faithful to God and thanking his parents, he had written something about me that shook me. He had written, "If it is decided for me to enter the heavens, I will be waiting for you." It was exactly the same words that he told me the night before his departure. How

---

33. Lady Fatimah al-Zahra (615-632) was the daughter of the Prophet (s), and the wife of Imam Ali.
34. *Fatimiyyah* days are the days on which Shias hold mourning rituals for the martyrdom of Lady Fatimah (a).

dumb could I be? He kept calling me and telling me that he loved me, but I was not smart enough to notice what he meant by it. I was not sad at his departure, just angry at myself that exactly at the point that I needed to pay more attention to him, I had closed my eyes to the signs. I was angry that I had not noticed that it was his time to go. If I had only realized it in time, I would have remembered all his actions. Then I would know what I was supposed to do and what the right thing was to do for me.

Ismail had a notebook where he wrote all his thoughts. For instance, he would write for himself, that he should not have carried a specific action or said a particular word. He would write down some punishments for himself. He was forcing himself not to repeat the same mistakes. All this would make me feel even worse.

There were a lot of people present at his funeral. I realized Ismail did not just belong to me; he belonged to all the people who got to know him since his childhood. Some of the troops in the Badr division would say, "We only allow it for him to be buried in Iran for a short period of time, so we can take him to Iraq once the war is over, as he belongs to our people and us." There were some people present at his funeral that did not look like his friends at all. His oldest friends and classmates from back at the university days had come to the funeral as well; even those who were known to have communistic beliefs. One of my university professors came from Tehran and attended his 40th day of memorial as well.

Those were really difficult days for me. For the sake of my children, I would try to stay strong and not cry in public. Ibrahim and Zahra were too young to fully comprehend the different aspects of the situation. I tried to shield them from the truth as I was worried it would depress and break them. However, somebody had told them the truth and I was not pleased. Ibrahim said, "These people keep saying that dad is dead." I replied, "Those people lie." Once the funeral and the following customs were finished, I returned to Tehran, as the children needed to attend their schools. There I started to teach them that, "Being martyred is different from simply passing away. The martyrs are still alive; they stay with God and can see us." During the summer of that year, we were granted a trip to Mashhad through the IRGC. It reminded me of my first trip to Mashhad with Ismail.

The IRGC members took Ibrahim to the holy shrine. Once he returned, he asked me, "You told us that the martyrs are all alive, then how come Imam Reza is buried in that Golden tombstone?" I answered, "It's true that his body is in the tombstone, but his soul is alive and living with God." I hated it if Ibrahim's first impression of death would be emptiness and an end to life's journey. He asked me so many questions that I took him to see Ismail's grave when we went back to Tehran. I was happy to see he could play there as well.

I did not have many problems continuing my life after his departure. Before his departure, I felt like I was already a martyr's wife because I did not really see him that often. I was used to making all the decisions on my own. It was like I had a dream through all those years, and it was over. Even my studies at the university had improved! I raised my children and made sure they were provided with a good life. It is what it is, and that is the way of life. Now I am looking forward for my turn, so he does not wait for too long before the open doors of heaven. Come to think of it; it is not that bad. Let him get the bitter taste of waiting and anticipation as I have grown used to living with its bitter taste.

www.ingramcontent.com/pod-product-compliance
Lightning Source LLC
Chambersburg PA
CBHW030043100526
44590CB00011B/312